BIG
BEASTS

Alligator

Stephanie Turnbull

Published by Smart Apple Media
P.O. Box 1329
Mankato, MN 56002

Printed in the United States of America,
at Corporate Graphics in North Mankato, Minnesota.

Designed by Helen James
Edited by Mary-Jane Wilkins

Library of Congress Cataloging-in-Publication Data

Turnbull, Stephanie.
 Alligator / by Stephanie Turnbull.
   p. cm. -- (Big beasts)
 Includes index.
 Summary: "An introduction on alligators, the big beasts in lakes
and rivers. Describes how alligators swim and walk, find food,
communicate, and care for their young. Also mentions how
they are different from crocodiles"--Provided by publisher.
 ISBN 978-1-59920-831-2 (hardcover, library bound)
 1. Alligators--Juvenile literature. I. Title.
 QL666.C925T87 2013
 597.98'4--dc23
                          2012004110

Photo acknowledgements
l = left, r = right, t = top, b = bottom
page 1 Miroslav K/Shutterstock; 3 Hemera/Thinkstock;
4 Perry Correll/Shutterstock; 5 Pamela McCreight/Shutterstock;
6 Brian Lasenby/Shutterstock; 7t choikh/Shutterstock, b RUDVI/
Shutterstock; 8 iStockphoto/Thinkstock; 9 Hemera/Thinkstock;
10 chloe7992/Shutterstock, 11 Bonnie Fink/Shutterstock;
12 Design Pics/Thinkstock; 13 iStockphoto/Thinkstock;
14-15 iStockphoto/Thinkstock; 16 Heiko Kiera/Shutterstock;
17 Heiko Kiera/Shutterstock; 18 Heiko Kiera/Shutterstock;
19 Lars Christensen/Shutterstock; 20 iStockphoto/Thinkstock;
21 Rudy Umans/Shutterstock; 22t Alexia Khruscheva/Shutterstock,
b Eric Isselée/Shutterstock; 23l AbleStock.com/Thinkstock,
r altrendo nature/Thinkstock
Cover Eric Isselée/Shutterstock

DAD0503
042012
9 8 7 6 5 4 3 2 1

Contents

Alligators are

gigantic!

Big and Bulky

Alligators are huge, heavy, meat-eating reptiles.

They have an enormous, strong tail and terrifying jaws.

Hard, bony plates protect their body.

Types of Alligator

Most alligators live in
swampy lakes and rivers
in southeast America.

A few alligators live in China. They are much smaller.

Alligators are not crocodiles! Crocodiles show their bottom teeth when their mouth is shut.

Alligators love
to be warm.
They spend hours
basking in the sun.

In winter, they dig
hollows in mud.
The holes fill with
water to make little
sheltered ponds.

On the Move

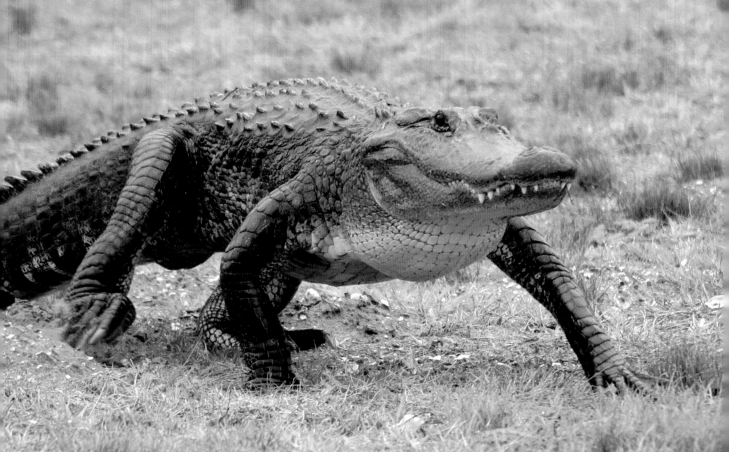

Alligators can walk with their body lifted high off the ground, or slither on their belly...

... but they are built for
SWIMMING!

Their long, flat tail
and webbed back
feet push them
through the water.

11

Hidden Killers

Alligators spend hours lurking
low in the water, as still as a log,
watching and waiting...

... then suddenly **lunge** at prey with wide open jaws.

SNAP! They gobble fish whole.

CHOMP! They bite into big animals, and drag them underwater.

13

Terrible Teeth

Alligators have about 80 pointed teeth that crunch through bone in a flash.

They sink their teeth
into large prey, then spin
and twist wildly to rip off
a bite-sized chunk.

15

Nests and Eggs

Female alligators lay about 35 eggs and bury them in soil and leaves to keep them warm.

Babies break out of their eggs after about nine weeks. New alligators are called hatchlings.

Stripy Babies

Young alligators are black
with bright yellow stripes.

Babies stick close to their mom—otherwise they might become a snack for hungry raccoons, birds, or even adult alligators!

Watch Out!

Alligators like to be left alone. If they feel threatened, they may attack with open jaws!

Sometimes they make low, rumbling **grrowwwls** in water. Their body shakes and the water fizzes and bubbles around them.

BIG Facts

Adult American alligators are longer than you and two friends lying end to end.

The biggest alligators weigh about the same as a racehorse.

American alligators are the largest reptiles in North America.

Alligators sometimes attack animals as big as Florida panthers and black bears.

Useful Words

lunge
To pounce or fall forward suddenly.

prey
An animal that is hunted by another animal.

reptile
A type of scaly animal that lays eggs. Alligators, crocodiles, snakes, and lizards are all reptiles.

Index

Web Link

Look at this coloring book of alligator facts and safety tips, made by children in Florida who live near alligators.
http://myfwc.com/media/310155/Alligator_AAA_booklet.